Mort Künstler's
CIVIL WAR

THE NORTH

Mort Künstler's

CIVIL WAR

THE NORTH

Mort Künstler

RUTLEDGE HILL PRESS

Nashville, Tennessee

Published in Nashville, Tennessee, by Rutledge Hill Press, 211 Seventh Avenue
North, Nashville, Tennessee 37219. Distributed in Canada by H. B. Fenn and Company, Ltd., 34 Nixon Road, Bolton, Ontario, Canada L7E 1W2. Distributed in the
United Kingdom by Verulam Publishing, Ltd., 152a Park Street Lane, Park Street,
St. Albans, Hertfordshire AL2 2AU. Distributed in Australia by Millennium Books,
33 Maddox Street, Alexandria, NSW 2015. Distributed in New Zealand by Tandem
Press, 2 Rugby Road, Birkenhead, Auckland 10.

Jacket and text design by Bruce Gore / Gore Studio, Inc.
Color separations by Patrick Wray Litho

Library of Congress Cataloging-in-Publication Data

Künstler, Mort.
   [Civil War]
   Mort Künstler's Civil War : the North / Mort Künstler.
     p.   cm.
   ISBN 1-55853-477-6
   1. United States—History—Civil War, 1861–1865—Pictorial works—
Catalogs.   2. United States—History—Civil War, 1861–1865—Art and the
war—Catalogs.   3. Künstler, Mort—Catalogs.   I. Title.
E468.7.K85 1997
759.13—dc21   97-9408
                                                              CIP

Printed in the United States of America
1 2 3 4 5 6 7 8 9—02 01 00 99 98 97

Especially for

MY DEAR TOMMY

☆ ☆ ☆

Contents

★ ★ ★

Introduction	8
The Flag and the Union Imperiled	10
The Waiting War	14
"Raise the Colors and Follow Me"	20
The Emancipation Proclamation	28
Grierson's Butternut Guerrillas	36
Last Leave	44
Col. Robert Shaw and the 54th Massachusetts	50
The Eve of Battle	56
Morning Riders	60
"Hold at All Cost!"	68
"There's the Devil to Pay"	78
Dilger at Gettysburg	86
Chamberlain's Charge	94
The High Tide	104
The Angle	114
"Keep to Your Sabers, Men!"	122
Veterans of Gettysburg	132
The Glorious Fourth	136
The Gettysburg Address	146
On to Richmond!	154
Sheridan's Men	162
The Bloody Angle	168
War Is Hell!	176
Lincoln's Inaugural Ball	184
Acknowledgments	192

Introduction

THE ORIGIN OF this collection of my work can be traced to two paintings. In 1982, I was commissioned by CBS to paint the first of my Civil War scenes, which became the official logo for the miniseries *The Blue and the Gray.* That work piqued my interest in the war and launched me on a journey during which I painted a number of Civil War paintings that were exhibited at Hammer Galleries in New York City in November 1982.

The second painting and perhaps the most important one, as far as this body of work is concerned, is *The High Water Mark.* In 1988, while I was in Gettysburg researching the painting, I wandered into American Print Gallery. By good fortune, I met Ted Sutphen, the owner. I learned that he and his wife, Mary, were the largest publisher of limited-edition military prints in the country. They were familiar with my work, and when I described the painting I was planning, they offered to publish it even though it had still not been done.

The Sutphens published *The High Water Mark,* and the original was unveiled at the Gettysburg National Military Park Museum by U.S. Sen. Alphonse D'Amato on the 125th anniversary of the battle. The print quickly sold out, and more than sixty-five limited-edition prints have followed.

The paintings in this book are a selection of my personal favorites that feature subjects from the war with a Northern viewpoint.

In the text that follows, I have explained in words and pictures the evolution of my paintings from concept to finished work. Each painting poses its own problems and solutions. They are not spontaneously created but demand time and care to germinate and grow. A thorough and well-planned process—including historical research, study of military tactics and equipment, and visits to the battle sites—is behind every work.

The famous are featured, from Lincoln and Grant to Sherman and Sheridan. Because the common soldier was the heart and soul of the Union army, I was equally interested in capturing Billy Yank on my canvas.

Some of the events portrayed are famous, like the battle of Gettysburg. Others, as in *Last Leave* and *The Waiting War,* capture moments of everyday life during the war. It is this sort of mix that I have always enjoyed painting.

Painting subjects from the Civil War has been a great adventure for me. I continue to be amazed by what I learn, and in this book I have tried to share some of my discoveries about a war that defined the meaning of freedom for generations to come.

The Flag and the Union Imperiled

CHARLESTON, S.C.
April 12, 1861

The idea for this painting came from my desire to paint the April 12, 1861, firing on Fort Sumter in Charleston Harbor in South Carolina, the beginning of the Civil War. At the same time, I wanted to show the Stars and Stripes under fire.

The fort's flagpole stood on the parade ground and normally would have been visible to the artillerymen on the parapet. At the start of hostilities, however, the Federal commander, Maj. Robert Anderson, ordered his men to the lower casemates, placing them out of sight of the flagpole I wanted to depict.

On further investigation, I found that Sgt. John Carmody, frustrated at being on the receiving end of the Confederate shelling, raced to the parapet against orders and fired the entire line

of previously loaded guns. His solitary act of defiance provided my moment for *The Flag and the Union Imperiled*.

From floor plans and maps of the fort I learned the positions of the guns fired by Sergeant Carmody. I portrayed this 32-pounder because this particular artillery piece and the flagpole would fit into my composition. The sergeant wears an artillery-man's uniform with red trim and crossed cannon on his kepi.

The flag was the most fun to paint. It appears softly because of the smoke and sea spray that filled the air that day. The original flag is preserved at Fort Sumter. A visit allowed me to note the correct alignment of the stars in the blue field, which had not been standardized at the time of the Confederate bombardment. I was also able to accurately portray the tears and holes in their exact places. This touch of authenticity is subtle, but I take great pride in the realism I achieved.

The Waiting War

Most people visualize battle scenes

or portraits of the great leaders when they think about the Civil War, and not the tedious hours of homesickness and camp life that dominated the everyday, mundane existence of average soldiers. In diaries and letters home, they complained of endless drilling, poor food, tenacious lice, and homesickness. They also complained of too much waiting.

After the tents were pitched and duties fulfilled,

soldiers found themselves with a lot of free time, and they filled these empty hours with a variety of homemade entertainment. Card games from cribbage to poker (called "bluff") and gambling over anything from the weather to louse races were favorite pastimes.

Other activities in camp included games, singing, and dancing. They played baseball, checkers, and tug of war. After a snowfall they had elaborate snowball fights, with officers drawing battle lines and issuing bugle calls. In summertime, swimming was highly valued, and soldiers from both sides sometimes shared the same swimming hole.

Music was heard in every camp, and most regiments included at least a violinist, a banjoist, or a bone player. The most popular songs in the Federal camps were "John Brown's Body," "Yankee Doodle," and "The Battle Cry of Freedom." Where there was music, there was dancing—even without women. Soldiers would request hoop skirts and bonnets from home so they could simulate women at regimental "balls."

Drinking was prevalent, and various kinds of home brew were concocted with such names as "Nock 'em Stiff" or "Oh, Be Joyful." Ultimately, the typical soldier would do anything to fend off the constant fear that the next battle might be his last.

In this painting, I illustrated a moment of camp life. The men have pitched their tents, hung their canteens, and leaned their weapons against makeshift tent poles. The underlying emotion is melancholy. The men pace or sit quietly, playing cards or whittling, all the while pondering if they will survive the next battle. For most men, the war represented the first great adventure away from home. As one soldier described it, the experience was "sheer boredom interspersed with periods of sheer terror."

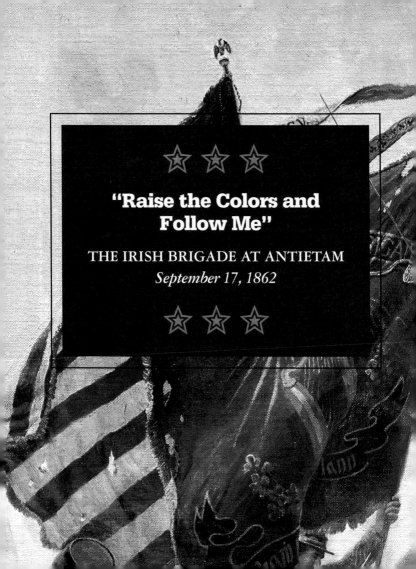

"Raise the Colors and Follow Me"

THE IRISH BRIGADE AT ANTIETAM
September 17, 1862

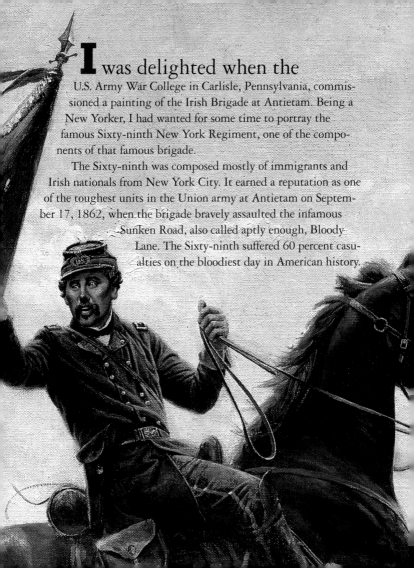

I was delighted when the U.S. Army War College in Carlisle, Pennsylvania, commissioned a painting of the Irish Brigade at Antietam. Being a New Yorker, I had wanted for some time to portray the famous Sixty-ninth New York Regiment, one of the components of that famous brigade.

The Sixty-ninth was composed mostly of immigrants and Irish nationals from New York City. It earned a reputation as one of the toughest units in the Union army at Antietam on September 17, 1862, when the brigade bravely assaulted the infamous Sunken Road, also called aptly enough, Bloody Lane. The Sixty-ninth suffered 60 percent casualties on the bloodiest day in American history.

I walked the entire battle line of the Sunken Road at the Antietam battlefield and through the fields the Union troops had crossed. For my purposes, the angle from the extreme right of the Union line offered the best view. The area slopes down and northeast, toward a farm, and I used this slope for my vantage point.

I timed my visit for September. Since I wanted to stage the scene between 10 o'clock and noon, I was there early in the morning. I used the rising sunlight to silhouette Gen. Thomas Francis Meagher, commander of the Irish Brigade, and both the U.S. and the famed green Irish Brigade flags. I showed the Confederate line to the south entrenched in the Sunken Road. Additional research confirmed that the Sixtyninth had been positioned to attack at this spot.

The troops are equipped with the Model 1842 musket and wear only their belt sets and canteens, having left behind their haversacks, knapsacks, and blankets. Meagher, astride the rearing horse, wears a Model 1850 staff-and-field sword. It

was one of four swords he owned and is now in the collection of the University of Notre Dame. His uniform and likeness are based on contemporary accounts and photographs.

During my research I met Ken Powers, the official historian of the Sixty-ninth, and Barney Kelly, the Sixty-ninth's Veterans Corps commander. Through their efforts, I found that the flag used at Antietam was preserved at the New York City Armory. The bright green flag had inspired reckless heroism during the battle; eight color-bearers died leading the Irish Brigade's attack at the Sunken Road. At one point the colors fell to the ground, and Meagher yelled over the din, "Raise the colors and follow me!"

Contrary to previous reports that the regimental flag had been inscribed with the words "69th Regiment Irish Brigade," the flag reads "1st Regt. Irish Brigade," meaning that the Sixty-ninth was the first regiment raised among the four regiments in the brigade. We also found that the flag was embroidered rather than painted, which was the usual practice at that time.

Because I planned to show the flag's reverse side, I had to decide whether to paint the flag authentically or portray it in a readable form, as if it were a painted flag. After consultation with historians from the Military History Institute, we decided on the more readable approach. I duplicated the original flag's exact lettering and design, adding the streamers precisely as they were. The bullet holes in the painting's flag correspond to the battle damage suffered by the original.

When Ken Powers and Barney Kelly came to my studio to see the almost-finished painting, imagine my surprise when I discovered they brought the actual finial from the top of the flagpole used during the battle. I cannot describe the thrill I felt holding it in my hands and, of course, matching the finial in the painting with it.

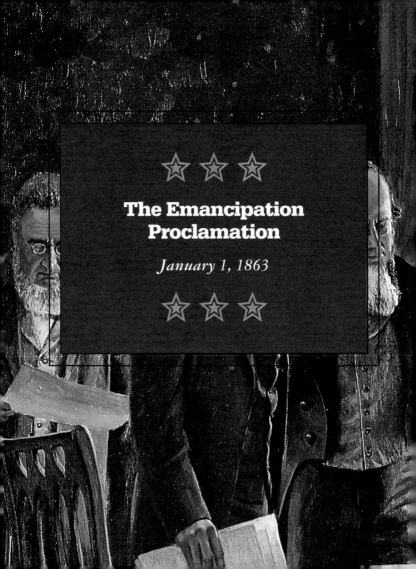

The Emancipation Proclamation

January 1, 1863

On New Year's Day 1863, Abraham Lincoln signed the Emancipation Proclamation and freed all slaves in the states then in rebellion against the Union. He later said, "If my name ever goes into history it will be for this act, and my whole soul is in it." With the stroke of his pen, he redefined the war as against and for slavery as opposed to the more abstract restoration of the Union.

A great deal of information, both written and pictorial, is available on this subject. Most of my visual information came

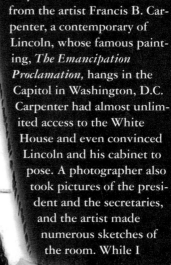

from the artist Francis B. Carpenter, a contemporary of Lincoln, whose famous painting, *The Emancipation Proclamation,* hangs in the Capitol in Washington, D.C. Carpenter had almost unlimited access to the White House and even convinced Lincoln and his cabinet to pose. A photographer also took pictures of the president and the secretaries, and the artist made numerous sketches of the room. While I

In giving freedom to the slave, we assure freedom to the free—honorable alike in what we give, and what we preserve. We shall nobly save, or meanly lose, the last best, hope of earth.

from Lincoln's 1863 State of the Union address

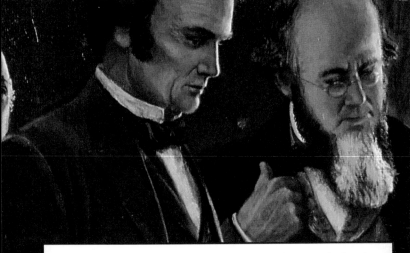

gained very little from his finished painting, Carpenter's sketch pad was a treasure trove of detail.

This project posed several unusual problems for me. My predicament was that while I easily learned the patterns and colors of the rug, wallpaper, and drapes, putting this information into perspective for my painting was tedious and laborious. Since I had seen Carpenter's finished picture, I tried not to duplicate his vantage point, making my task that much harder.

After the usual number of thumbnail and preliminary sketches, I began a detailed line drawing, which I used to solve these problems, particularly that of perspective. This pencil drawing alone took more than eight days. The likenesses were relatively easy since there are many photographs of Lincoln and his cabinet. The chairs in the painting are still in the White House today, having been found and restored to the mansion by First Lady Lou Hoover. The lighting fixture is based on Carpenter's sketches.

Detailed pencil drawing

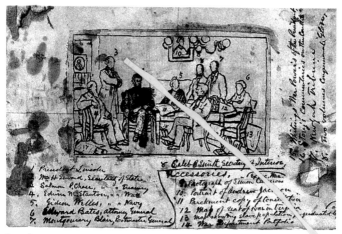

Page from Carpenter's sketchbook

The Emancipation Proclamation *by Francis B. Carpenter*

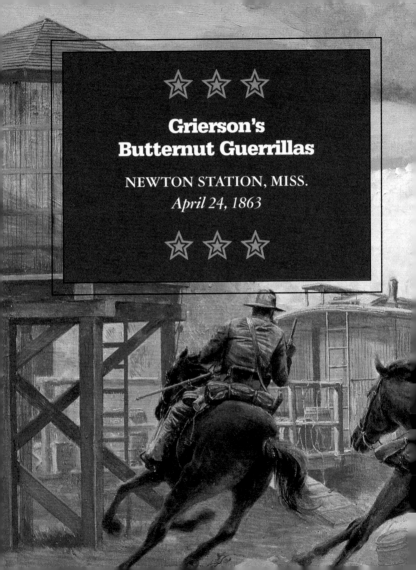

Grierson's Butternut Guerrillas

NEWTON STATION, MISS.
April 24, 1863

In April 1863, U. S. Grant employed two major diversions to breach the daunting barriers around Vicksburg. One was a feigned attack near the Yazoo River. The other, Col. Benjamin Grierson's cavalry raid behind enemy lines, is the subject of this painting.

On April 17, when Grierson led a force of seventeen hundred cavalrymen out of La Grange, Tennessee, his orders were to disrupt communications, destroy supplies, and cause as much mischief to the enemy as possible while deceiving them as to the identity and size of his force. Called Grierson's Butternut Guerrillas because some of them dressed as Confederate irregulars, the Federals duped unsuspecting Confederates, and by April 24 had penetrated two hundred miles into enemy territory.

That same day, Grierson sent a scouting party to Newton Station, Mississippi. They rode in quietly that morning, posing as Confederates, and they could not have been more lucky. A westbound freight train, headed for Vicksburg with ordnance and commissary supplies, had pulled into a siding to allow an eastbound train from Vicksburg to pass on the main track. The cavalrymen surprised the Confederates, seized both trains and destroyed everything, blowing up the locomotives, ripping up the track, and burning the warehouses, the station, and other outbuildings. By 2:00 P.M. the troopers had finished their work and fled the town.

This scene takes place in the morning hours. The incoming train appears with the sun behind it, and the cavalrymen spring into action.

The signal flags hanging from the station house windows indicate the siding is clear for the westbound train, while the red flag notifies the engineer that a train is approaching from the opposite direction. The equipment and the men's uniforms are both Confederate and Union, as was described in contemporary accounts of the raid.

When he entered the Union lines at Baton Rouge, Louisiana, Grierson reported one hundred enemy killed and wounded and more than five hundred captured. There were only twenty-six Union casualties. His men destroyed as much as sixty miles of railroad and telegraph lines, confiscated supplies headed to Vicksburg—both ordnance and commissary, and captured more than a thousand horses and mules. Truly remarkable, even by John Wayne standards!

Grant claimed the sixteen-day, six-hundred-mile raid was a complete success. The Federal commander did not usually use superlatives, but he later described Grierson's raid as one of the most brilliant cavalry exploits of the war.

Last Leave

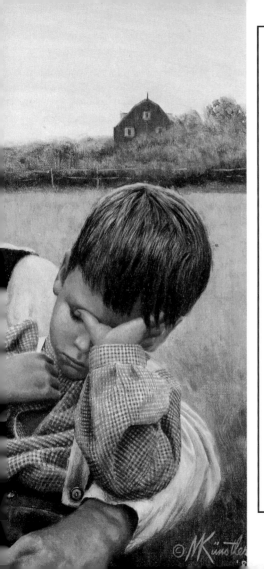

I painted
Last Leave at about the same time as *The Waiting War*. It was supposed to be a painting of a father just before he returns to his unit; I wanted to capture a melancholy mood similar to *The Waiting War*.

The soldier could be any father. The quiet landscape around him is vastly different from the war-torn world that demands his return. He cradles his young son, whose innocence is untouched by the terrors of war. As the man stares into the distance, it is as if he tries to see the future. Will he ever see his family again? Will he return crippled? Will his son remember him if he does not return? Would this, indeed, be his last leave?

As many as 2.2 million men left their homes and loved ones to serve during the Civil War. Although the largest age group that served was composed of young men less than twenty-one years old, Northern volunteers aged from pre-teens to the elderly fought and died to preserve the Union.

Conceptual sketch

Col. Robert Shaw and the 54th Massachusetts

BOSTON

May 28, 1863

The 1989 movie *Glory* presented the story of the famous Fifty-fourth Massachusetts Infantry and inspired me to do this painting. The Fifty-fourth Massachusetts was the first all-volunteer African-American regiment recruited in the North. It was authorized by Gov. John Andrews, who envisioned it as a model regiment of former slaves and freedmen. Among the recruits were two of Frederick Douglass's sons, Charles and Lewis. The son of a prominent abolitionist family, Col. Robert Gould Shaw, was appointed to command the regiment, whose founding was controversial as not all white Northerners believed in the fighting abilities of African Americans. The Fifty-fourth became a model of perfection in drill and camp. When the Fifty-fourth completed its training and marched through Boston

on May 28, 1863, to embark for the South Atlantic theater, Massa-chusetts Gov. John Andrew presented the colors to Shaw with the words: "I know not, Mr. Commander, when in all human history, to any given thousand men in arms there has been committed a work at once so proud, so precious, so full of hope and glory as the work committed to you. I stand as a man and a magistrate, with the rise or fall in history of the Fifty-fourth Massachusetts Regiment."

On July 18, 1863, the Fifty-fourth found fame following a brave but suicidal assault on South Carolina's Battery Wagner, which was a sand fort less than two miles from Charleston's Fort Sumter. Shaw and almost half the regiment were killed during the attack. Shaw was buried in an unmarked grave with the rest of the casualties.

Following Shaw's death, Col. Edward N. Hallowell assumed command of the Fifty-fourth. The unit remained based in South Carolina for the remainder of the war and was used in operations in Georgia and Florida, most notably at the February 20, 1864, battle of Olustee, Florida.

There are several good photographs and portraits of Shaw, so his likeness was rather easy to capture. I based the enlisted men on many period photographs of African Americans in uniform. Since the regimental flag of the Fifty-fourth is in the collection of the Commonwealth of Massachusetts, I was able to portray it accurately.

The Eve of Battle

GEN. J. BUFORD
Gettysburg
June 30, 1863

During my involvement with the
adaptation of Michael Shaara's novel *The Killer Angels* by
Turner Entertainment as the movie *Gettysburg*, I was reminded
of the vital role Gen. John B. Buford played in the early hours
of the battle. To my knowledge, his story had never been
depicted in a painting.

Lee's army was marching
through Maryland and into
Pennsylvania, but the Union
army, undergoing another
change in command,
was not sure of the
whereabouts of the

Confederates. Lee too was unsure of the disposition of the Federal army. Both sides were probing for the other.

On June 30, 1863, Buford was at the head of two brigades of Union cavalry that arrived in Gettysburg in search of Lee's invading army. Commanding the only Federals in the area, he knew that he had to secure a defensive position when the Confederates attacked.

I wanted to portray the trying moments of decision that Buford experienced on the eve of the three-day battle. Knowing that the next morning he would face the entire Confederate army with only two brigades, he could only try to delay the tide of gray until the rest of the Union army arrived. That evening he chose to occupy McPherson's Ridge, hoping it would provide effective cover and give some advantage to his outnumbered men.

A simple composition of this type demands that every element be just right. Buford's figure has to reflect all of the emotions he might have felt the night before the battle. The angle of his head, his stride, and the way he holds his field glasses must be meaningful.

The two basic elements in this painting are Buford and his headquarters at the Lutheran Seminary. I utilized the design elements of the vertical (Buford) opposed to the horizontal (the seminary building). The diagonal line of his sword complements the horizontal and vertical shapes. The light in the window heightens the tension and suspense as Buford ponders the possibilities of the next day.

Morning Riders

GEN. J. BUFORD
Gettysburg
July 1, 1863

There was a heavy mist on the Pennsylvania countryside at dawn on July 1, 1863. Buford and his entourage left his headquarters early that morning and headed northwest to inspect the line along McPherson's Ridge.

I was looking for a moment that had not been painted before. When I learned of the morning mist on July 1, I immediately focused my attention on Buford's early morning actions.

The general rides a black horse and is followed by a trooper carrying

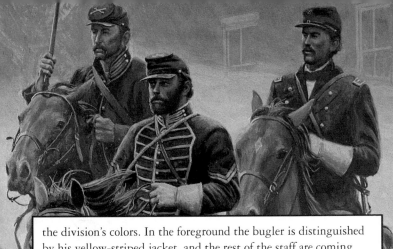

the division's colors. In the foreground the bugler is distinguished by his yellow-striped jacket, and the rest of the staff are coming out of the mist.

The view is of the west side of the Lutheran Seminary. The building that was used as Buford's headquarters still exists, but the windows, chimneys, and facades have changed over the years. Even so, the building itself has changed little since 1863. Thus it was relatively easy to observe the sunlight on the seminary cupola in the early hours of the day. It rises over Culp's Hill and strikes the cupola first, which gave me an opportunity to take advantage of an unusual lighting effect.

I was fascinated with my subject while working on this painting. The architecture and the lighting were a challenge, and again I had an opportunity to portray Buford at one of the critical moments prior to the battle of Gettysburg. His foresight in choosing a strong defensive position came into play repeatedly throughout the three-day engagement and would ultimately decide the fate of not only the battle, but the outcome of the war.

Conceptual sketch

"Hold at All Cost!"

GEN. J. BUFORD

Gettysburg
July 1, 1863

Buford's decision to make a determined stand against the oncoming Confederates at Gettysburg cannot be underestimated. His decisive action set the stage for the battle that seemed to hold the outcome of the war in the balance.

On the morning of July 1, 1863, elements of Confederate Gen. Henry Heth's brigade approached the town from the west. His men were in search of supplies, particularly shoes, which were rumored to be warehoused in Gettysburg. Heth had expected to meet some resistance, possibly even state militia. Thus his men were taken off guard when they encountered Buford's battle-ready horse soldiers.

They will attack you in the morning and they will come booming—skirmishers three deep. You will have to fight like the devil to hold your own until supports

arrive. The enemy must know the importance of this position and will strain every
nerve to secure it, and if we are able to
hold it, we will do well.

John Buford, July 1, 1863

In the painting, Buford and his staff have taken positions behind the dismounted cavalrymen on McPherson's Ridge, behind a small stone wall and some rail fencing. The firing has just begun at long range, as evidenced by the raised rear sights on the troopers' Sharps carbines. In portraying Buford's men, I wanted to show a long defensive line in a long, narrow composition that would accommodate as many cavalrymen as I could paint.

Since these first shots were fired at McPherson's Ridge, I visited the site to study the ground and the buildings. There I found the barn reconstructed on its original site for the national park.

With his men in a strong defensive position and the Confederate attack under way, Buford has done his job. He wears a sack coat with a black velvet collar, which enabled me to add some authentic and human touches, such as the watch chain and pipe.

I faced a challenge in showing several cavalrymen up close. The problem is that all the troopers are dressed more or less alike and use the same weapons, which tends to make the picture boring. To address this problem, I emphasized the differences in their faces and varied their poses and uniforms wherever possible. I placed the visor strap on their caps in every conceivable way it could be worn. A few caps also show the crossed-sabers cavalry insignia.

This scene shows almost every component of a Federal cavalry brigade—the commanding officer and staff, the horse soldiers on the front line, and the unit's guidon. The number ones on the red and white bars of the flag indicate that this detachment is part of the First Division of the First Corps.

While the acrid smoke of battle filled the air, Buford could only hope that his men would hold their ground until reinforcements arrived. With his attention focused on the enemy, others would have to take notice of any approaching aid from Union infantry.

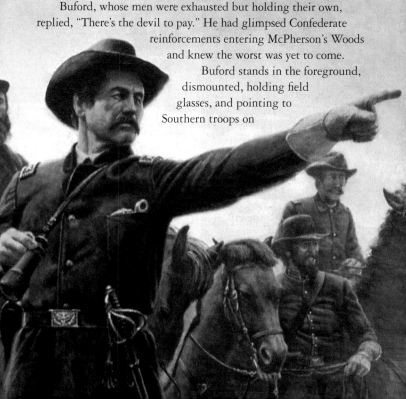

Outnumbered three to one, Buford's men held Heth's Confederates at bay while Gen. John F. Reynolds and the Union First Corps infantry raced across the Pennsylvania countryside. They arrived at Gettysburg shortly before ten o'clock that morning, two hours after Buford's engagement had begun.

The title of the painting is based on Buford's reply to Reynolds's initial question, "What's the matter, John?"

Buford, whose men were exhausted but holding their own, replied, "There's the devil to pay." He had glimpsed Confederate reinforcements entering McPherson's Woods and knew the worst was yet to come.

Buford stands in the foreground, dismounted, holding field glasses, and pointing to Southern troops on

the other side of Willoughby's Run. Reynolds peers through his glasses, taking in the scene and confirming Buford's information.

The action occurs on McPherson's Ridge, with the farmer's barn in the background and to the right. Two fieldpieces mark the left and right sides of the painting. Both are 3-inch ordnance rifles, part of Lt. John Calef's Battery A, Second U.S. Artillery. They were positioned here and remain there to this day. In the background, a shell bursts near one of the troopers holding the reins of his unit's horses while he leads them to a safe area beyond the ridge.

Buford, casual in his field appearance—note the unbuttoned collar of his four-button sack coat—has his ever-present pipe in his chest pocket. His guidon is carried by the mounted corporal immediately behind him, and his horse is held by the dismounted sergeant seen immediately below his outstretched arm.

Reynolds is on a black charger. He has a western-style saddle, which is preserved at the MOLLUS Museum in Philadelphia. A brace of pistols in horse holsters is attached to the saddle. Reynolds's uniform is regulation dress for general officers, with the buttons grouped in threes and a velvet collar and cuff. Directly behind him is his headquarters flag, which I based on the image in the second volume of *Headquarters Flags.* A fragment of the actual flag is also in the MOLLUS Museum in Philadelphia.

Reynolds's cavalry escort was Company L of the First Maine Cavalry. Their guidon flies between the two headquarters flags. The other flag in the painting is the artillery guidon of Calef's battery, with the lieutenant seen mounted to the immediate right of the guidon and directly behind the artillery piece in the left foreground. The officer directly to Reynolds's left is Capt. Myles Keogh, one of Buford's aides; he died in 1876 with George Custer at the Little Big Horn.

Dilger at Gettysburg

July 1, 1863

The two armies took most of the first
day just to gather at Gettysburg. During that time, units went into
action as soon as they found the town, and by noon the Union line
was manned by two corps, the First on the left and two divisions of
the Eleventh on the right. By
midafternoon, however, the line
was beginning to buckle under
the Confederate onslaught.

In the action of that afternoon,
Capt. Hubert
Dilger, one of
the foremost
artillerists in the
Union army, ordered two of his guns
forward of the main battle line without infantry support. This type of
bold action was unheard of at the
time, and it is the moment
depicted in this painting.

Under fire, Dilger
orders a section of
two guns for-
ward to a more
advantageous
position
against the
Confederate
guns on Oak

Hill. The section's lieutenant guides the off-lead horse, which is shying from the gunfire. A corporal with the battery guidon rides next to the lead driver. Six horses pull the limber that tows the cannon, and behind them is the caisson. Each gun usually had a crew of ten. Dilger's second gun follows on the right.

In laying out the painting, I studied various angles and researched harnesses, saddles, gun carriages, and implements. Artillerymen faced tremendous danger in this sort of maneuver, being completely exposed as they directed the six-horse team.

Dilger's deployment occurred over open farmland that was mostly wheat field and pasture. In the lower right corner shells have scorched the ground, and small fires have begun.

The section made its courageous move at about four o'clock that afternoon, and sunlight can be seen breaking through the heavy smoke to the right, or west, of the picture. The two artillery pieces to the far right are where the battery was posted originally, and the battery's monument stands there today.

In the background is the Old Dorm of Pennsylvania College—now known as Gettysburg College. The building stands today basically unchanged, but because of the town's growth, it is difficult to see the dormitory from where Dilger's men stood. The small field where his section charged, however, has been preserved.

Dilger's men were exceptional, and his battery performed well, but it had little effect against the Confederate attack that afternoon. Later his men heroically held off Southern infantry by themselves, giving retreating Union troops sufficient time to form a secondary line of defense on Cemetery Hill.

The special danger artillerymen faced during the war has often been underestimated, and *Dilger at Gettysburg* is my tribute to these unsung heroes.

Chamberlain's Charge

LITTLE ROUND TOP

Gettysburg
July 2, 1863

Little fighting occurred during the morning and early afternoon of the second day at Gettysburg. The late afternoon made up for it, however. Confederates attacked both sides of the Union line, which had pulled back southeast of the town. The right side was anchored at Cemetery Hill, and the left ended at the two hills known as the Round Tops.

As the Union line consolidated, word came to Union commander Gen. George Gordon Meade's headquarters that there were no troops on the Round Tops and the hills were unprotected. Realizing that his line could be enfiladed if the Round Tops fell into Confederate hands, Meade ordered all available troops to the hill known as Little Round Top.

One of these units was the Twentieth Maine Regiment, commanded by Col. Joshua Lawrence Chamberlain. An unlikely commander, Chamberlain had been a professor of rhetoric at Bowdoin College before the war.

Almost as quickly as Chamberlain's men occupied the crest of Little Round Top, they came under attack. Wave after wave of Confederates attempted to dislodge the Maine men, but Chamberlain's Twentieth held, although they suffered high casualties.

As his ammunition ran out, Chamberlain ordered an unlikely maneuver—a charge. With fixed bayonets, the Twentieth proceeded downhill. The exhausted Confederates were stunned, some firing their weapons and then surrendering. In a matter of moments, the Twentieth had taken more than four hundred prisoners. Little Round Top held, and the position was reinforced.

The painting illustrates Chamberlain's charge late in the afternoon of July 2, 1863. The sunlight filtering through the wooded round top focuses attention on the heroic professor-turned-warrior as he leads the Twentieth Maine down the southwestern slope of the hill. The large boulder in the foreground is still a prominent landmark at the scene of the charge. The trees depicted in the painting are different than what is found on the slope now, but today's forest is a mixture of old and new growth, just as it was in 1863.

The red Maltese Cross on the cap of the color bearer identifies him as a member of the First Division of the Fifth Corps. The "20" on his cap denotes the Twentieth Maine, and the national flag was the only banner the regiment carried into battle that day. The dent in Chamberlain's scabbard shows where it deflected a bullet that day—a deflection that saved him from a serious wound.

I hope this painting captures some of the drama, excitement, and heroism of that critical moment at Gettysburg.

Composition sketch

Conceptual sketch

Watercolor study

The High Tide

Gettysburg
July 3, 1863

The battle of Gettysburg climaxed with the assault against the center of the Union line—commonly called Pickett's Charge. Approximately fifteen thousand Confederate soldiers formed a line almost a mile long and marched across a field almost a mile wide to attack. In conceiving *The High Tide*, I wanted to show the charge in a different way from a previous painting, *The High Water Mark*, which offered a Confederate perspective.

By looking from the south to the north, I could show the Confederates

charging from the left instead of the right. I focused more tightly on the scene to narrow the panoramic view I had used in my previous version. Dropping the eye level also gave the painting a different perspective. The close-range fighting in the Angle and along the stone wall that traced across Cemetery Ridge makes the scene easily recognizable to most viewers as Gettysburg.

In the chaotic action portrayed here, several units of Virginia infantry have reached the stone wall, but the Federals' concentrated fire takes a deadly toll. The Southerners who succeeded in breaching the wall are quickly cut down.

Pickett's Charge failed to break the Union center, and a vital part of Lee's three-pronged strategy failed. The Confederacy lost as many as half the men who crossed the bloody fields below Cemetery Ridge.

Most of the flags shown in this painting are standard Confederate battle flags, with the Ninth Virginia Infantry seen in the center and the Fiftieth Virginia Infantry in the background. To the right is the regimental flag of the Seventy-second Pennsylvania and the state-issued flag of the Seventy-first Pennsylvania. The Seventy-second was a semi-Zouave regiment, but many of its men had worn out most of their distinctive uniform, except for the low white canvas gaiters distinguished by the four buckles on each side, which can be seen on two of the soldiers in the right background. The cloverleaf and number "69" on the kepi of the soldier in the right foreground identify him as a member of the Sixty-ninth Pennsylvania.

The Angle

Gettysburg
July 3, 1863

I conceived of *The Angle* after I had done *The High Water Mark,* which illustrated Pickett's Charge from a Southern point of view. I wondered how I could stage this scene differently from the way many other artists had painted it. I looked at my own painting of *The High Water Mark* and decided to portray everything from the opposite direction by reversing my view. While the view in *The High Water Mark* was from above, looking down and to the south from

the north, in *The Angle* the scene is drawn at eye level from the south looking north. This created a reverse angle picture. It brought the action in the far background of *The High Water Mark* into the foreground and allowed me to show intense hand-to-hand fighting in detail. It also enabled me to place the Union and Confederate flags close to each other.

During Pickett's Charge, the fighting at the stone wall along Cemetery Ridge turned to hand-to-hand combat. The Angle was a winding section of the wall where some of the most desperate fighting of the war occurred. It was here that a few hundred Tennesseans and Virginians penetrated the Federal line and here that they were immediately cut down or captured.

While I thought I had thoroughly explored Pickett's Charge, my involvement with Turner Entertainment's film *Gettysburg* led me to paint every step of the infamous charge in a series that appeared in the companion book to the movie. One result of that labor is that I continue to be intrigued by the battle, and I am sure I will be drawn back to it in the future.

"Keep to Your Sabers, Men!"

GENS. CUSTER AND HAMPTON

Gettysburg

July 3, 1863

This picture was my first print in
the *Killer Angels* portfolio, a series I based on the battle of Gettysburg. I wanted it to be a scene that had never been painted before. It
needed to be an action piece, and it needed to include both Northern and Southern forces. When I read of the cavalry clash between
Confederate Gen. Wade Hampton and Union Gen. George Arm-
strong Custer on July 3, 1863, I knew I had found my subject.

On the third day at
Gettysburg, the Confed-
erates attempted a
coordinated assault
against the Federals
from three direc-
tions. While

Pickett's Charge focused on Cemetery Ridge, Lee's cavalry moved to the Union left. The plan called for the charge to break through the Union center and a portion of the cavalry to pressure the Federal flank. The remaining cavalry would strike the Federals from the rear.

At about 3:30 in the afternoon, just as the survivors of Pickett's Charge had begun retreating from the Union center, the two cavalry forces charged headlong at each other. Twenty-three-year-old Custer, at the time the youngest general in the Union army, led his Michigan brigade with the now famous battle cry, "Come on you Wolverines!"

The Confederate cavalry's traditional weapon of choice at close quarters was firearms, but in this action sabers—the preferred weapon of the Union cavalry—were used. At the head of his troops, Hampton was heard to shout above the din, "Keep to your sabers, men! Keep to your sabers!"

Both cavalries galloped fearlessly toward each other, with the Union moving northeast and the Confederates southwest. The sun was in the west, behind the Southerners. Federal artillery fired on the Confederates, but their galloping line continued undaunted. When the two sides hit, some said that the impact was heard a mile away. Horses tumbled over each other, end over end.

Initially, the advantage was with the South, but Federal pressure on the Southern flanks crumpled their formation. The Union left flank held, and the Confederates pulled back, ruining any chance for a successful attack against the rear of the Northern line. Hampton was badly wounded in the melee, and Custer was credited by some with personally capturing Hampton's battle flag.

Conceptual sketches

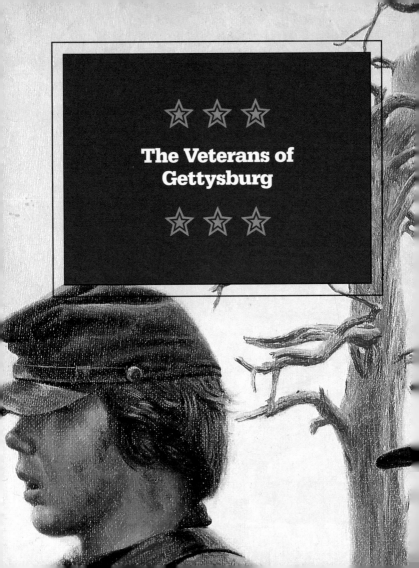

The Veterans of Gettysburg

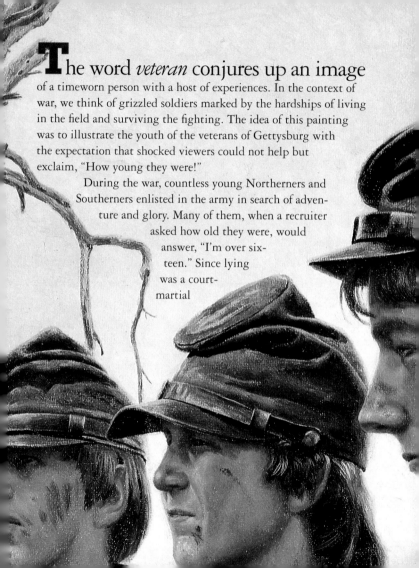

The word *veteran* conjures up an image of a timeworn person with a host of experiences. In the context of war, we think of grizzled soldiers marked by the hardships of living in the field and surviving the fighting. The idea of this painting was to illustrate the youth of the veterans of Gettysburg with the expectation that shocked viewers could not help but exclaim, "How young they were!"

During the war, countless young Northerners and Southerners enlisted in the army in search of adventure and glory. Many of them, when a recruiter asked how old they were, would answer, "I'm over sixteen." Since lying was a court-martial offense, the boys would write the number sixteen on a piece of paper and place it in their shoe so they would literally be "over" sixteen. Most recruiters winked at this dodge and processed the boys with the other enlistees. Needless to say, they encountered all the unimagined horrors, mutilation, and death that war had to offer.

In this painting, four youngsters stand in the calm that followed the battle of Gettysburg. The dirt and scratches on their faces, hands, and uniforms and the battered tree in the background are all signs that a battle has just occurred. The boys hold their weapons and gaze over the battlefield. Their eyes reflect a mixture of relief and grief—relieved to be survivors and grieved at the sheer horror they have witnessed for the past three days.

The Glorious Fourth

GEN. U. S. GRANT
Vicksburg
July 4, 1863

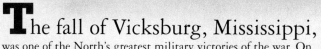

The fall of Vicksburg, Mississippi, was one of the North's greatest military victories of the war. On July 4, 1863, one day after the Union victory at Gettysburg, Confederate Gen. John C. Pemberton surrendered the Mississippi River stronghold, relinquishing more than sixty thousand small arms, almost two hundred cannon, and thirty thousand soldiers. With this victory, the North won complete control of the river. Ulysses S. Grant later said, "The fate of the Confederacy was sealed when Vicksburg fell."

When I became familiar with the Vicksburg siege, I felt the surrender was excellent material for a painting. I consulted historians, studied maps and photographs, reviewed the literature and records of the battle, and visited the U.S. Navy Memorial Museum in Washington, D.C.

After forty-seven days of siege, Pemberton believed

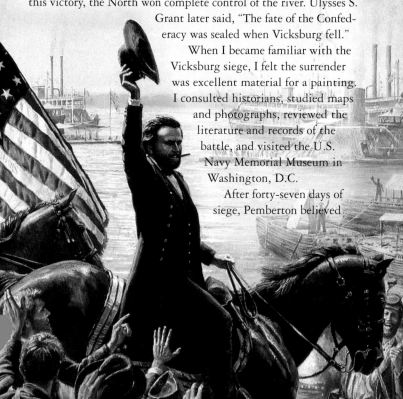

that he would obtain the best surrender terms by capitulating on July 4, the anniversary of the signing of the Declaration of Independence. At 10:00 A.M., he relinquished the city to the Federals. Grant and his entourage were en route to a meeting with Adm. David Porter, commander of the river fleet, and passed through a flag-waving, cheering crowd of eight thousand Union troops as they celebrated their Fourth of July victory at the Old Landing.

The painting shows Grant just before his meeting aboard Porter's flagship, the USS *Benton*. The admiral can be seen on the extreme left of the top deck, on the steps to the pilothouse.

The key to a picture this complex is to capture the celebratory nature of the moment and still lead the viewer's eye to Grant. Atop his favorite mount, Cincinnati, the general is in his typical informal dress with no sword belt, acknowledging the cheers of the crowd. In his party, immediately behind him, are Gens. John D. Stevenson, James B. McPherson, and John C. Logan. These three likenesses were difficult to master because I could not find photographs of any of the three generals in the positions in which they are portrayed here.

I learned that regiments from Illinois, Indiana, Minnesota, and Wisconsin were present, and their presence is indicated by the lettering on the battle flags. The flags of the Forty-fifth Illinois and the Fourth Minnesota, which both claimed to have been the first to enter the city, are shown prominently. The shieldlike symbol on the top of the forage cap of the soldier behind the cart on the extreme left and on the hat of the soldier in the wagon on the far right attest that they are members of the Seventeenth Corps. A few sailors can be seen in the crowd and immediately behind Grant's mount.

Although Grant's orders called for the Federals to appear in full uniform, it was a hot summer day in Mississippi, and many of the soldiers are in shirt sleeves. I recalled the old saying that a Civil War soldier obeyed any reasonable order, not because it was an order, but because it was reasonable.

Empty buckets and barrels in and beside the cart in the foreground are symbolic of the shortages that forced the city to surrender after the twelve-week siege. The few civilians present are old men—like the farmer on the wagon—women, and children. A small group can be seen in the extreme left background, sullenly observing the festivities. Behind them in the upper left corner of the picture is the Warren County Courthouse flying a Union flag. The courthouse, the only building in the painting that still stands today, is now a museum.

The flagship of the river fleet, the *Benton* is the ship in the forefront on the far right. The topmost flag with the star on the mainmast is a headquarters flag. The red, green, and blue pennant immediately below it is the ship's identification pennant. The colorful signal flags spell out congratulations and greetings and are based on information from Preble's *History of the Flag*.

All ships, rams, monitors, and converted riverboats in the background represent the vessels that were present at the ceremony. Directly behind the *Benton* is a typical riverboat that was converted into a fighting vessel when the war began. The other four ships in the background, from right to left, are the USS *Choctaw*, a double-turreted Monitor-class gunboat (two of which were at Vicksburg), Gunboat Number 53, and Gunboat Number 54.

The Glorious Fourth is by far the most difficult and time-consuming painting I have ever done. An interesting postscript is that I finished the painting on July 4, 1989, exactly 126 years after the event. It was truly a glorious Fourth for me!

The Gettysburg Address

November 19, 1863

On November 19, 1863, at the dedication of the national cemetery at Gettysburg, Abraham Lincoln delivered the most famous speech in history. He spoke for less than two minutes, but his eloquent words have reverberated through the years. In the midst of dedicating a cemetery, the president rededicated the purpose for the war, calling not for a Union victory, but for the preservation of the nation as a whole.

The dedication was well covered by the press and well attended by the public, with estimates of those in attendance varying between fifteen and twenty thousand. Most of them were there to see the president.

In spite of this crowd, very little visual information is available to help an artist portray the event accurately. Few pictures were taken that day, and there is only one known photograph of the president at the dedication. I consulted chief park historian Kathy Harrison and historians John Heiser and Bob Prosperi to learn as much as I could about the ceremony.

*F*our score and seven years ago our fathers brought forth on this continent, a new nation, conceived in Liberty, and dedicated to the proposition that all men are created equal. Now we are engaged in a great civil war, testing whether that nation, or any nation so conceived and so dedicated, can long endure. We are met on a great battlefield of that war. We have come to dedicate a portion of that field, as a final resting place for those who here gave their lives that that nation might live. It is altogether fitting and proper that we should do this. But in a larger sense, we can not dedicate—we can not consecrate—we can not hallow—this ground. The brave men, living and dead, who struggled here, have consecrated it, far above our poor power to add or detract. The world will little note, nor long remember what we say here, but it can never forget what they did here. It is for us the living, rather, to be dedicated here to the unfinished work which they who fought here have thus far so nobly advanced. It is rather for us to be here dedicated to the great task remaining before us—that from these honored dead we take increased devotion to that cause for which they gave the last full measure of devotion—that we here highly resolve that these dead shall not have died in vain—that this nation, under God, shall have a new birth of freedom—and that government of the people, by the people, for the people, shall not perish from the earth.

The speeches were delivered from a platform, and while there is no record of their exact position, it is known that flags were positioned behind the speakers. The principal speaker, Edward Everett, and Secretary of State William Seward shared the platform with the president. Everett sits at the extreme left. There was little difficulty in portraying these two dignitaries since they were widely photographed at different times. In the far background, wearing white sashes, are six of the seventy-two mounted marshals designated to control the proceedings. The water pitcher and glasses are placed in front of the speakers more on the basis of conjecture than fact.

The greatest challenge, after gathering my information, was the crowd. For variety, some of the men are shown without hats. In each case, I have placed a woman near or behind each man. I imagine several men were asked to remove their hats that day so the ladies could see the president. Still, it is difficult to paint so many faces, especially if each person is treated individually, and my crowd work seemed endless.

Of course, portraying Lincoln was not a problem and even a pleasurable task. When called upon for a few appropriate words, he read the address from two folded papers—rather than the mythical back of an envelope. When he concluded, he was distressed by the audience's lack of reaction. Some have suggested that the people were surprised by the two-minute address, having just stood through Everett's two-hour speech. Other reactions were mixed, some complimentary, some critical, and the president was convinced the speech had been a failure.

As time passed, however, the importance of his message was recognized. In his succinct and reverent manner, Lincoln had redefined the war effort, not in terms of conquest and defeat, but as the promise of "a new birth of freedom."

On to Richmond!

GRANT IN THE WILDERNESS
May 7, 1864

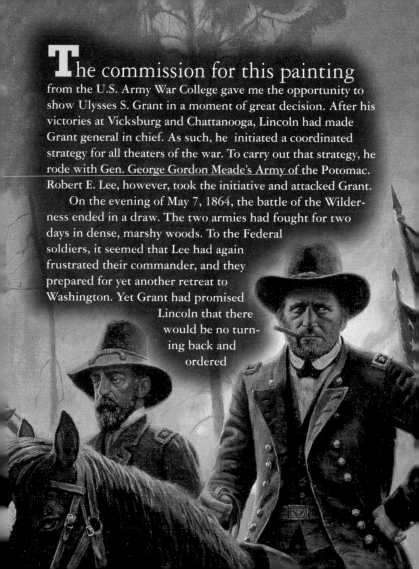

The commission for this painting from the U.S. Army War College gave me the opportunity to show Ulysses S. Grant in a moment of great decision. After his victories at Vicksburg and Chattanooga, Lincoln had made Grant general in chief. As such, he initiated a coordinated strategy for all theaters of the war. To carry out that strategy, he rode with Gen. George Gordon Meade's Army of the Potomac. Robert E. Lee, however, took the initiative and attacked Grant.

On the evening of May 7, 1864, the battle of the Wilderness ended in a draw. The two armies had fought for two days in dense, marshy woods. To the Federal soldiers, it seemed that Lee had again frustrated their commander, and they prepared for yet another retreat to Washington. Yet Grant had promised Lincoln that there would be no turning back and ordered

his army south to Richmond rather than north in retreat. His men, realizing that their efforts had not been in vain on this battlefield, cheered spontaneously. The cycle of defeat and retreat under all their old commanders had been broken.

Because fire and smoke covered the battlefield that dark night, I heightened the drama by showing Grant close in the foreground. Meade, the hero of Gettysburg, is alongside. The debris of war is everywhere as the soldiers applaud their commanders.

Directly to Grant's right is Meade's headquarters flag, which is documented in *American Military Equipage*. Its color is described as solferino, which is a vivid, purplish pink, and the design was of a golden eagle encircled by a silver wreath. Grant was said to have remarked on first seeing it, "What's this? Is Imperial Caesar anywhere about here?"

The Fifth Corps, marching with knapsacks, gives way to the generals and their staffs. The infantryman in the extreme right foreground wears the identity pin of the Fifth Corps on his chest.

The men dug in behind the barricade are from the Second Corps, which is indicated by the shamrock corps badges on the forage caps of the two men kneeling and sitting in the extreme left front. The blue corps badges on their caps denote the Third Division. A knapsack from the Fifty-seventh Pennsylvania is in the background.

Although the battle was a statistical draw, the Union's unimpeded movement toward Richmond was a strategic victory. As the Federal army headed south, these soldiers realized there was something different about Grant. After years of being led into retreat by a succession of generals—Irvin McDowell, George B. McClellan, John Pope, Ambrose E. Burnside, and Joseph Hooker—they finally had a commander who would lead them on to Richmond.

Sheridan's Men

When Grant gave Philip Sheridan

command of the Army of the Potomac's cavalry, Sheridan reshaped these horsemen into the Union's most effective weapon. Earlier in the war, the cavalry had been the weakest branch of the service, and its Confederate counterpart had taunted and tortured the Federals with speed and skill. Sheridan's goal was to use the cavalry as a striking force. By 1864 he was close to achieving that goal.

Sheridan was a short, fiery man with a hot temper. Throughout the spring of 1864, his men wreaked havoc on Southern rails and supply wagons. In May, he mounted a raid near Richmond,

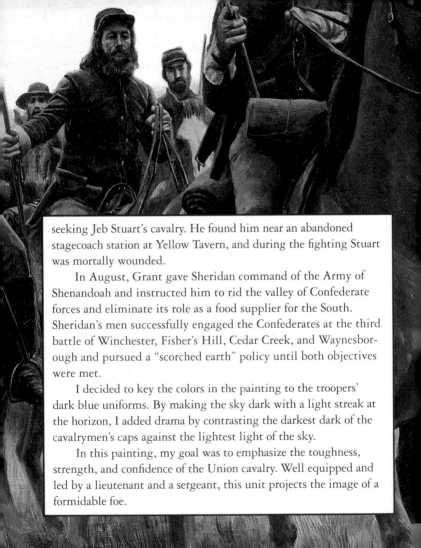

seeking Jeb Stuart's cavalry. He found him near an abandoned stagecoach station at Yellow Tavern, and during the fighting Stuart was mortally wounded.

In August, Grant gave Sheridan command of the Army of Shenandoah and instructed him to rid the valley of Confederate forces and eliminate its role as a food supplier for the South. Sheridan's men successfully engaged the Confederates at the third battle of Winchester, Fisher's Hill, Cedar Creek, and Waynesborough and pursued a "scorched earth" policy until both objectives were met.

I decided to key the colors in the painting to the troopers' dark blue uniforms. By making the sky dark with a light streak at the horizon, I added drama by contrasting the darkest dark of the cavalrymen's caps against the lightest light of the sky.

In this painting, my goal was to emphasize the toughness, strength, and confidence of the Union cavalry. Well equipped and led by a lieutenant and a sergeant, this unit projects the image of a formidable foe.

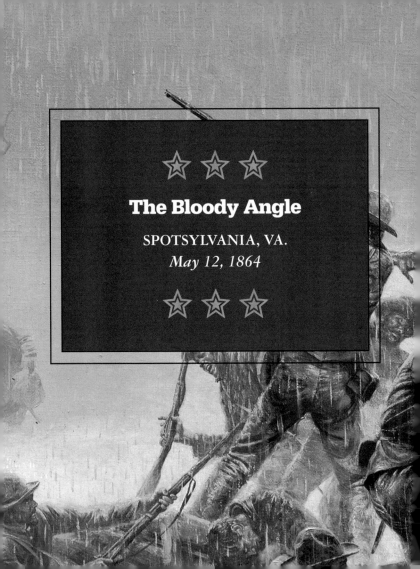

The Bloody Angle

SPOTSYLVANIA, VA.
May 12, 1864

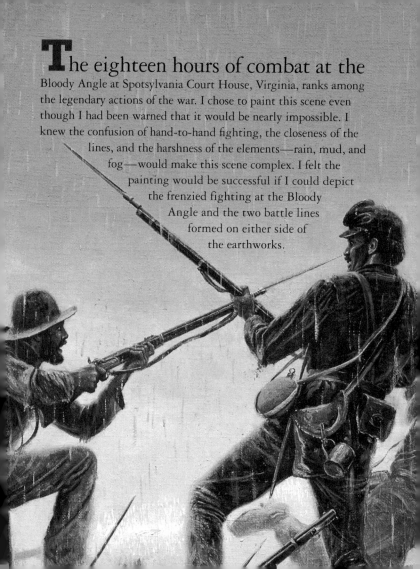

The eighteen hours of combat at the

Bloody Angle at Spotsylvania Court House, Virginia, ranks among the legendary actions of the war. I chose to paint this scene even though I had been warned that it would be nearly impossible. I knew the confusion of hand-to-hand fighting, the closeness of the lines, and the harshness of the elements—rain, mud, and fog—would make this scene complex. I felt the painting would be successful if I could depict the frenzied fighting at the Bloody Angle and the two battle lines formed on either side of the earthworks.

Grant's march on Richmond had been delayed. To continue farther into Virginia, his army had to break through the Confederate defenses around Spotsylvania Court House, the strongest and most elaborate system of trenches and earthworks seen in the war to that date. Five and a half feet of earth was piled in front of the Confederate trenches, which were divided into pens about twelve to eighteen feet wide to prevent enfilading fire if the Federals broke the line.

The fighting that occurred here was horrific. One Federal soldier said, "It was the most terrible day I have ever lived."

The worst fighting took place in an angle in the log-and-earthen wall. Called the Bloody Angle, this two-hundred-foot section was littered with bodies, sometimes two or three deep. Wounded men suffocated in the mud and drowned in the flooded trenches. Firing occasionally ceased for men to clear the corpses from the trenches so the riflemen would have a better footing. Large oak trees were cut down by the continuous fire, frequently crashing down on the ranks in the trenches. The mud and blood mixed to turn the trenches into sticky, horrific graves.

In the painting, Union Col. Oliver Edward's brigade, identified by the white cross on their caps, smashes into Confederate Gen. Robert Rodes's Virginians at the west angle. Union soldiers try to top the fallen log while Confederates fire from behind it. The muddy floor of the trench is piled with bodies. Fog obscures the landscape in the background, and the light is diffused. With only a few feet of earthworks separating them, the soldiers' acts of desperation became commonplace.

In a painting of this type, I feel successful if the desperation and horror these valiant men felt comes across to the viewer. I can think of no more desperate moment for either Northerner or Southerner than the kill-or-be-killed muddy melee at the Bloody Angle.

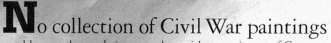

No collection of Civil War paintings would come close to being complete without an image of Gen. William Tecumseh Sherman. Along with Sheridan, he rounds out the circle of Union leadership initiated by Grant as general in chief. My only problem was determining how and when to portray him.

In a speech after the war, Sherman said, "There is many a boy here today who looks on war as all glory, but, boys, it is all hell." Over time that has been shortened to "War is hell." Few people would know better than Sherman, for it was he who brought the hellish torch to the Deep South in 1864.

Like Sheridan's scorched-earth policy in the Shenandoah Valley, Sherman's view of war dictated that the conqueror consume, burn, or destroy anything that might contribute to the enemy's ability to wage war. He realized that this included the

destruction of civilian property as well as military assets, which would debilitate the South and facilitate a Union victory.

Because the burning of Atlanta has been immortalized for many people in the film version of *Gone with the Wind,* I was drawn to place this scene in that context. I began by placing Sherman on horseback, looking back at the city in flames from a rise in the countryside. Then I remembered his famous quote and thought about hell and decided to dramatize the scene by making it fiery.

After many sketches, I decided to use the fire as my main light source. Unfortunately, I knew of no way to include Sherman. That is, until I took another look at Burke Davis's book *Sherman's March to the Sea.*

I learned that on the night of November 15, as the fires raged, the Federals began leaving the city. How could I place Sherman in the picture when he did not leave until the next day? While some thought that he was watching the fire from his headquarters, further research indicated that he was in the street, directing troops in extinguishing the fires that threatened private homes. With this information, I chose to depict Sherman with his troops in the city.

The raging fires provide drama and light, while the scorched remains of chimneys, nicknamed Sherman's Sentinels, give mute testimony to the devastation.

The keys to this painting are, of course, the lighting effect in the background and Sherman in the center. The general's determined personality is suggested by the jaunty angle of his ever-present cigar. The final painting includes the elements of the burning of Atlanta, dramatic lighting, Sherman, and units of his army. It is as close as I could come to portraying "Uncle Billy's" most famous quote: "War is hell!"

Lincoln's Inaugural Ball

March 4, 1865

I based this painting of Lincoln's second inaugural ball on a Major-and-Knapp lithograph that was published by Frank Leslie in 1865. The inauguration took place on March 4, 1865. The president rode by carriage from the White House to the Capitol, where he and Vice President Andrew Johnson were sworn in by Chief Justice Salmon P. Chase. After the appropriate speeches, an escort of cavalry, bands, and spectators led the presidential party back to the Executive Mansion.

Newspapers reported that Lincoln shook hands with more than six thousand people at the reception that followed. In the painting he is accompanied by his wife, Mary, as he makes his way to the main ballroom where even more people wait to congratulate him. Vice President Johnson is directly

With malice toward none, with charity for all, with firmness in the right as God gives us to see the right, let us finish the work we are in, to bind up the nation's wounds, to care for him who shall have borne the battle, and for his widow and for his orphans, to do all which may achieve and cherish a just and a lasting peace among ourselves and with all nations.

from Lincoln's second inaugural address

★ 187 ★

behind him, and to the right are Gen. George Gordon Meade, Secretary of State William Henry Seward, and Attorney General Edward Bates. The uniformed figure to the left of the president is Gen. Ulysses S. Grant.

The mantle, clock, and candelabra are based on items that were in the White House at the time. I portrayed the president with tired eyes but slightly smiling. Perhaps he knew his work would soon come to an end. In the Emancipation Proclamation he had freed the slaves. In his address at Gettysburg he had rededicated the war effort to the nation's founding ideals. In his Second Inaugural Address he encouraged the nation to "bind up its wounds…with malice toward none." Perhaps his smile was born of a hope for a renewed nation that would cherish liberty and peace.

Within a month's time Lincoln would sit at Jefferson Davis's desk in the Confederate White House in Richmond and Lee would surrender at Appomattox. Ultimately, in a tragedy for the reunited nation, the president would be shot on the evening of April 14, losing his life as the war was ending. The man who had carried the nation through four years of war and brought it successfully back to its founding principles would be sorely missed through the painful era of Reconstruction. Some say he was the last casualty of the war.

With special thanks to:

Larry Stone and Ed Curtis of Rutledge Hill Press who originated the idea of twin volumes of my Civil War paintings. Their imagination and expertise have brought to fruition *Mort Künstler's Civil War: The North* and its companion book on the South.

Richard Lynch, director of Hammer Galleries in New York City, who gave me my first one-man show in 1977. Nine more shows and a lasting friendship have followed. My appreciation also to Howard Shaw and the rest of the staff at Hammer Galleries.

Ted and Mary Sutphen of American Print Gallery, Gettysburg, Pennsylvania, who published my first Civil War print in 1988. More than sixty-five editions have followed. I treasure their advice and friendship and look forward to our future collaborations.

The myriad of historians, too numerous to mention on this page, who have all been so generous with their time and have enthusiastically shared their expertise and knowledge to ensure the accuracy in my paintings.

Jane Künstler Broffman and Paula McEvoy who continue to run a busy studio with dedication, patience, and understanding. I could not function without them.

And, my dear Deborah—wife, partner, consultant, adviser, lover, and best friend, who does everything possible to allow me the most time for my second love, painting.